RELIGIONS OF THE WORLD

I Am
Lutheran DISCARD

❧ ERICA BRADLEY ❧

The Rosen Publishing Group's

PowerKids Press™

New York

Published in 1999 by The Rosen Publishing Group, Inc.
29 East 21st Street, New York, NY 10010

First Edition

Book Design: Erin McKenna and Kim Sonsky

Photo Credits: p. 4 © Stefan Lawrence/International Stock; pp. 7, 8 © Corbis-Bettmann; p.12 © Chuck Mason/International Stock; pp. 15, 20 © Scott Thode/International Stock; p. 16 © Ron Chapple/FPG International.

Bradley, Erica.
    I am Lutheran / by Erica Bradley.
        p.   cm. — (Religions of the world)
    Summary: A young Lutheran boy introduces the history, beliefs, and practices
of this Christian religion.
    ISBN 0-8239-5263-0
    1. Lutheran Church—Juvenile literature. [1. Lutheran Church.] I. Title. II. Series: Religions of the world
(Rosen Publishing Group)
BX8065.2.B68 1998
284.1—dc21
                                                                    98-20145
                                                                     CIP
                                                                      AC

Manufactured in the United States of America

Contents

1	Michael	5
2	Martin Luther	6
3	An Historic Protest	9
4	American Lutherans	10
5	Born Again	13
6	Baptism	14
7	God's Words	17
8	Going to Church	18
9	The Lord's Supper	21
10	Lutherans Around the World	22
	Glossary	23
	Index	24

Michael

My name is Michael. My family is Lutheran, which means we believe in **Lutheranism** (LOO-ther-en-izm). Lutheranism is part of the Christian religion. All of Christianity is based on the teachings of a man named Jesus Christ. But different Christians believe in different ideas. Many Christians are either Catholic or Protestant. **Protestantism** (PRAH-tuh-stant-izm) is made up of people who belong to many different **faiths** (FAYTHS), such as Presbyterians, Baptists, or Methodists. Lutherans were the first Protestants.

◀ There are millions of Lutherans all over the world.

Martin Luther

Lutheranism gets its name from its founder, Martin Luther. Luther lived in Germany during the sixteenth century. At that time, almost everyone in Europe belonged to the Roman Catholic Church, including Luther. He carefully studied Catholic teachings and **beliefs** (buh-LEEFS). He decided he didn't agree with many of the Church's ideas. He and a few other people felt they had to reform, or change, religion as it was then. This period of time was called the **Reformation** (REH-for-MAY-shun).

Martin Luther left the Catholic Church to form Lutheranism. ▶

An Historic Protest

In 1517 Luther wrote down some of his ideas and posted them on the door of a big church in Germany. The writings were his **protest** (PROH-test), or disagreement, against the Catholic Church. Luther's actions of protest are where the word Protestant comes from. The leaders of the Catholic Church were very angry with him, but he didn't care. Luther continued to write down more and more of his ideas. These ideas were the beginnings of Lutheranism.

◀ Martin Luther worked hard to win his own religious freedom.

American Lutherans

Lutheranism started in Germany, but it quickly spread to other European countries. Around 1640, a small number of Lutherans came to America from Sweden. On arriving, they learned that they weren't welcome. They didn't speak English, which made things very difficult for them. Also, the Europeans who were already there didn't like the fact that the Lutheran religion was different from theirs. Soon, many Lutherans were put in jail, and others joined new churches. About one hundred years later, German Lutherans began to arrive in America and Lutheranism started to grow.

In order to practice the religion they wanted, Lutherans left Germany and traveled to America. ▶

DENMARK

BALTIC SEA

NORTH SEA

POLAND

NETHERLANDS

GERMANY

BELGIUM

CZECH REPUBLIC

LUXEMBOURG

FRANCE

AUSTRIA

SWITZERLAND

Born Again

Many Christians believe that people are born in **sin** (SIN). This means people aren't naturally as good as they should be. Martin Luther believed that the only way to lose this natural sin is through God's love. When this happens, a person is "reborn," or "born again." If someone is reborn, it means that she is closer to the type of person that Christians believe God wants her to be.

◄ Prayer is one way that Lutherans become closer to God and the kind of Christian they want to be.

Baptism

Lutherans also believe in **baptism** (BAP-tiz-um). During baptism, a person is dipped in or sprinkled with water. Baptism is a **symbolic** (sim-BAH-lik) way of washing away our sins and being reborn to a new life. The water used in baptism represents the acceptance of God's love. Lutherans believe we need His love to lose the natural sins with which we start our lives. Then we can begin life again.

Baptism is a time of holiness and celebration for many Lutherans. ▶

God's Words

The Bible is made up of two main sections, the Old Testament and the New Testament. The Old Testament is the story of the Jews. The New Testament tells about Jesus and Christianity. The Bible was written by many different people. But Lutherans believe that God spoke to these special people, who wrote what God told them. We believe that the words of both the Old and New Testament are actually God's words. The Bible is our guide for how to live and what to believe.

◄ Christians often turn to the Bible for help with the problems in their lives.

Going to Church

Every Sunday, my family goes to church together. The **pastor** (PAS-ter) leads the church services. He always starts by reading from the Bible. Then he talks about what the words mean and what they have to do with our lives today. After his sermon, which is a speech about God, everyone sings **hymns** (HIMZ). Another part of the service that usually follows the sermon is the Lord's Supper.

During a church service, a pastor will often stand at the altar, which is at one end of the church. ▶

The Lord's Supper

Lutherans and many other Christians share a **tradition** (truh-DIH-shun) that we call the Lord's Supper. This isn't an actual meal. Instead, we sip a little bit of wine and eat a small piece of bread. The wine and bread are supposed to be the blood and body of Jesus, or the Lord. The Lord's Supper brings us closer to God and to Jesus, who we believe is the Son of God. Some Protestants call the Lord's Supper the **Eucharist** (YOO-kuh-rist), or the Holy Communion.

◀ The Lord's Supper is a time for Lutherans and all Christians to remember Jesus and his death.

Lutherans Around the World

Lutherans don't live in only Europe and America. They are teaching people all around the world about Martin Luther's ideas. Today, there are Lutheran churches in countries like Brazil and Japan. In fact, not only is Lutheranism the first Protestant faith, but it's also one of the biggest. Of course, not all Lutherans **worship** (WER-ship) in exactly the same way. But no matter where we live, we all believe in the words of the Bible and the need for faith in God.

Glossary

baptism (BAP-tiz-um) The practice of symbolically washing away sins with water.

belief (buh-LEEF) Something that is believed.

Eucharist (YOO-kuh-rist) Another name for the Lord's Supper.

faith (FAYTH) A belief and trust in God.

hymn (HIM) A song that praises God.

Lutheranism (LOO-ther-en-izm) A Protestant faith based on the teachings of Martin Luther.

pastor (PAS-ter) A minister in charge of a church.

protest (PROH-test) An act of disagreement.

Protestantism (PRAH-tuh-stant-izm) A religion based on Christian beliefs which includes many smaller groups.

Reformation (REH-for-MAY-shun) A period of time in the sixteenth century where people rejected the beliefs of the Roman Catholic Church and turned instead to the Protestant Church.

sin (SIN) A wrongdoing.

symbolic (sim-BAH-lik) Representing something important.

tradition (truh-DIH-shun) A practice that is handed down from one person to the next.

worship (WER-ship) To pay great honor and respect to something or someone.

Index

B
baptism, 14
beliefs, 6, 13, 17, 22
Bible, 17, 18, 22

C
Christianity, 5, 17
Christians, 5, 13, 21
churches, 9, 10, 18, 22

E
Eucharist, 21

G
God, 13, 14, 17, 18, 21, 22

H
hymns, 18

J
Jesus Christ, 5, 17, 21
Jews, 17

L
Lord's Supper, 18, 21
Luther, Martin, 6, 9, 13, 22
Lutheranism, 5, 6, 9, 10

P
pastor, 18
prayer, 13

protest, 9
Protestantism, 5, 9, 21, 22

R
Reformation, 6

S
sermon, 18
sin, 13, 14
symbolic, 14
symbols, 21

T
tradition, 21

W
worship, 22